Happy Teachers' Day 2023

Thank you for being my
teacher.

this journal belongs to

Mrs. Charity Pitton

From: Elijah

Date

May 12, 2023

JOEL OSTEEN

THE POWER OF
FAVOR

JOURNAL

When you honor God,
when you keep Him first place,
you will find favor
in the eyes of the Lord.

Introduction

*W*hat God has in your future can't be accomplished on your own. There are places He's going to take you that you can't get to by yourself. There will be obstacles that look too big, dreams that seem impossible. You're going to need assistance for where you're going.

The good news is, God has put something on you that gives you an advantage, something that will open doors that you can't open, something that will make you stand out in the crowd. It's called "favor." Favor will cause good breaks to come to you. Favor will take you from the background to the foreground. It wasn't a coincidence. That was the favor of God.

With quotes from the book *The Power of Favor*, this journal provides a great place to respond to the book, to keep track of the "coincidences" of favor in your life, or to simply journal about life and dream about the future.

The favor on your life will cause the right people to show up.

*T*he Creator of the universe is about to endorse you.

You may have some obstacles, situations that are unfair. That doesn't mean you don't have favor. Challenges come to us all, but favor is why you're not going to stay down. Favor is why you're going to rise back to the top.

*H*e's going to do things that are out of your league,
things you couldn't make happen.

*F*ather, thank You for endorsing me today.

*G*od wants to make you an example of His goodness, and if
you will walk in humility and always give God the credit,
there's no limit to how high He will take you.

Favor is more powerful than your résumé.

Expect doors to open for you that may not
open for somebody else.

You ou need to hold your head high and start expecting
to stand out in the crowd.

*W*hy don't you start carrying yourself like
you're a child of the King?

God wants to show you an abundant increase of His favors.

You have favor at work, favor at the grocery store, favor at the gym, favor in traffic, favor at the mall.

*W*hen something good happens, recognize that it's the favor of God
and then learn to thank Him for it.

*W*hen you live favor-minded, it's like a bright light
shining down on you.

*Y*ou are glowing with God's goodness.
You are radiating with God's favor.

*W*hat will defeat others won't be able to defeat you.

*I*f God allows it to happen, He's promised that He will
turn it somehow and use it for your good.

$\mathcal{W}$e may have things around us that could harm us,
keep us from our dreams, bring us down. Stay in faith.

Dare to pray bold prayers. Believe for unusual favor.
Take the limits off God.

*W*hen you don't see how you can accomplish your dreams, don't get discouraged. You have a supply line connected with good breaks, the right people, ideas, and creativity.

*L*ike the Israelites, God has put a distinction on your life.

*G*od is about to do some things in your life that are
going to get you noticed.

$\mathcal{W}$herever you go, the blessing goes.

*Y*ou're not doing life alone. You have the most powerful force in the universe breathing in your direction right now.

*W*hen it comes to favor, you're not a lightweight. You are heavy with favor. You are weighted down with God's goodness.

This is your time to rise higher, to come into overflow, to see those dreams come to pass.

*G*od wants to do something that you've never seen,
something out of the ordinary.

*W*hen you dream big, believe big, expect big,
God will supersize what you're dreaming about.

*W*hen you know you're heavy with favor,
you'll see God do amazing things.

Believing is the key.

*G*od is about to show out in your life. Get ready for breakthroughs, for promotion, for healing, for a new level of your destiny.

*G*od's favor will accelerate things. It's not going to take as long as you think to accomplish your dreams.

*Y*ou are the apple of [God's] eye. He wants to
show you His goodness.

*E*very morning, you need to declare, "I have the favor of God."

*H*aving favor doesn't mean you won't have challenges.
Favor is what's keeping those challenges from defeating you.

There is a force working for you in the middle of the storm that is greater than any force that's trying to stop you.

*W*e have favor when we're in between walls of water.
We have favor when enemies are chasing us.

....
....
....
....
....
....
....
....
....
....
....
....
....
....
....
....
....
....
....
....
....
....
....
....
....
....

Freedom is coming.

God od can increase you in spite of what's going on around you.

*F*avor is what's going to catapult you to a new level.

$\mathscr{Y}$ou may not see a way, but God has a way.

*I*t may look as though you're stuck, but you can't see
what's happening behind the scenes.

Unexpected blessings are coming your way.

God has favor waiting for you, ideas waiting for you,
the right people waiting for you.

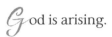

*G*od is arising.

*G*od is fighting your battles, causing you to stand out,
bringing you from obscurity to notoriety.

*W*hat God lifts up, no person can push down.

*I*t's fa...time. It's healing time. It's acceleration time.
It's blessing time.

*Through your eyes of faith, you have to see God arising,
fighting your battles, moving obstacles out of your path,
preparing the way for you to step into a new level of your destiny.*

You don't have to figure it all out. All you have to do is believe.

When it's your set time, all the forces of darkness
cannot hold you back.

*T*here should be people you're in relationship with who inspire you,
who challenge you, who make you strive to do better.

*W*hen you recognize the favor on a person's life, and you respect that favor by connecting with it, by honoring them and learning from them, that favor will come back to you.

The anointing you respect is the anointing you will attract.

You don't have to compete with people. You don't have to try to outperform them. You're not in competition with anyone except yourself. Let where they are inspire you to be the best that you can be. As iron sharpens iron, they can sharpen you. They can make you better.

*W*hen you keep God first place, you're connected
to a supply line that will never run dry.

*I*f you just say, "God, all I have is this little bit of oil, all I have is mustard seed faith," then watch what God will do.

....

....

....

....

....

....

....

....

....

....

....

....

....

....

....

....

....

....

....

....

....

*R*eceive this into your spirit: Healing is flowing, strength is flowing, restoration is flowing, freedom is flowing.

*H*e not only knows what you need,
but He knows when you're going to need it.

*C*all on the name of the Lord and He will answer you.

You're going to walk into favor that you've never seen, into opportunity, healing, abundance, and new levels of your destiny, in Jesus' name.

*E*veryone will see His hand on your life.

*H*e's a supernatural God. Get ready, He's about to burn up some rocks. He's about to move what looks permanent. It's not just going to surprise you; it's going to surprise the people around you.

*I*t's good to read about God's power, it's good to talk about it, it's good to remember it, but God wants you to experience it.

He's about to do something unprecedented.
Get ready for new ground. Get ready to go
where you couldn't go on your own.

$\mathcal{Y}$ou're the difference maker. You can be the one to affect
your family line for generations to come.

Your past is not going to limit you.

....
....
....
....
....
....
....
....
....
....
....
....
....
....
....
....
....
....
....
....
....
....
....
....

*W*ear your blessings well.

You keep honoring God, being your best. He will open doors
you never dreamed would open.

*G*od has decided to bless you.

People may rule you out, they may tell you it's never going to work out, but God has the final say.

*Y*ou're going to step into new levels and
see His favor in greater ways.

*G*od has already arranged good breaks for you,
things that you couldn't make happen.

....

....

....

....

....

....

....

....

....

....

....

....

....

....

....

....

....

....

....

....

....

....

*Y*ou don't need everyone to be for you. You just need
the right people to be for you.

*G*od is going to cause you to be seen in a new light.

The Most High God, the Creator of the universe, the One who spoke worlds into existence is breathing in your direction.

The right breaks will track you down. The right opportunities will come knocking at your door.

[God has] promised He will work out His plan for your life.

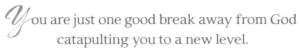

*Y*ou are just one good break away from God
catapulting you to a new level.

....
....
....
....
....
....
....
....
....
....
....
....
....
....
....
....
....
....
....
....
....
....
....

*P*itch your tent in the land of hope. Give God something
to work with. That's not just being positive.
That's your faith being released.

You ou may not see anything changing yet, but stay in faith, you are closer than you think.

*Y*ou cannot give God something without Him
giving you more back in return.

Just because you don't see a way,
doesn't mean God doesn't have a way.

By this time next year, you're going to be amazed
at where you are.

Your time is coming.

*W*hen you believe, things begin to change in your favor.

*W*e serve a supernatural God.

*W*hen God commands you to be blessed, He doesn't check
what family you come from, where you work, who likes you,
or how good the economy is. None of that matters to God...
When He commands the blessing, all the forces of
darkness cannot stop Him.

All the circumstances may be against you,
but the Most High God is for you.

The commanded blessing will override every person
who's tried to stop you.

You don't have to go after the blessing; go after God. Honor Him with your life, and the blessing will follow.

*I*f you could see where God is going to take you, the people
He's going to bring, the doors He's going to open, and the influence
He's going to give you, it would boggle your mind.

[God's] about to command increase, command abundance, command healing, command freedom upon you, in Jesus' name.

....

....

....

....

....

....

....

....

....

....

....

....

....

....

....

....

....

....

....

....

....

....

This is a new day. God's doing a new thing.
He's about to exceed your expectations.

Just because you gave up doesn't mean God has given up.

*O*ur attitude should be, *Lord, thank You that You're going to visit me again. Thank You that You're going to do more than I ask. Thank You for exceeding my expectations.*

Stay encouraged. God is not only going to bring you out, He's going to have some spoils there. There is going to be some plunder. He's going to bring you out better than you were before.

*Y*ou're asking for the possible; He's about to do the impossible.

You may have big challenges, but we serve a big God.
Your enemies may be powerful,
but our God is all-powerful.

*G*od has unlimited power. One touch of His favor
can turn a situation around.

Freedom is coming. Now get in agreement with God.
He's waking it up, so don't let it go back to sleep. Stir up your faith.
Believe that it's on the way. Go out with expectancy.

$\mathcal{I}$ know God has beauty for these ashes.
I know favor is in my future.

There never was a day of miracles; there's a God of miracles.

....
....
....
....
....
....
....
....
....
....
....
....
....
....
....
....
....
....
....
....
....
....
....

*W*hen you take the limits off God and dare to believe for
your dreams, don't be surprised if people try to talk you out of it.

Believe big, dream big, and pray big.

[*G*od] wants to make you an example of His goodness so that
everywhere you go, you don't even have to say anything—
your life is a testimony.

*G*od is not looking for religion. He's looking for people who simply
believe in Him, who know He controls the universe,
who believe He can do the impossible.

$\mathcal{G}$od is saying, "You don't have to fight these battles in your own strength. I'm going to go before you and clear the path. I'm going to make things happen you couldn't make happen. I'm going to defeat your enemies for you."

*W*hat you're up against may be bigger, stronger, more talented, and have more resources, but you're not on your own.

At the right time [God's] going to take you into your
Promised Land. That victory is on the way.

Those dreams you've given up on, those promises you've let go of, you need to get them back. They're not dead; they're just asleep.

*W*hen you live with this expectancy...that's when you'll see
explosive blessings that catapult you to the next level.

When [God] speaks, Red Seas part, blind eyes open, dreams come back to life.

[*G*od] said... "You may be satisfied, but I'm not satisfied. I'm going to do more than you asked."

[*G*od] knows what you're going to need. [God] knows
who you're going to need.

*W*hy don't you put your faith out there?

[G̶od's] idea of abundance is more than we can ask or think.

*I*t may seem like just another ordinary day, the same old thing,
everything looks routine. No, get ready.

The Scripture says when we have faith the size of
a mustard seed, nothing is impossible.

*I*t's your time to be free. It's your time to break bondages.
It's your time to go to new levels.

We think ordinary; God thinks extraordinary.

[God's] going to bring the fish to your nets.

Just keep God first place and let down your nets.
This commanded blessing, like a magnet,
will draw in good breaks, healing, favor, the right people.

....

....

....

....

....

....

....

....

....

....

....

....

....

....

....

....

....

....

*H*onor [God] with your life, and the blessing will follow.

*G*od will command things to find you.

People will tell you what you're not going to be, how you're not going to get well, how your dreams aren't going to come to pass. Here's the key: They can speak defeat all day long, but they are powerless to change the blessing on your life.

*T*he blessing always overrides the curse.

Tell the enemy, "You want me to curse my future? I know better.
I'm going to bless my future."

You know every force that's trying to stop you is powerless to change the blessing God put on your life.

All that matters is that God put His blessing on you
and everything else is of no effect.

*G*od will cause people to be good to you who have never been good to you. He'll use even your enemies to bless you.

All through the day, thank [God] that He's working in your life.

You have to let the seed take root. Here's the key: Don't talk yourself out of it. Talk yourself into it.

$\mathcal{L}$et God be your vindicator.

Stay in peace.

God is still on the throne. He hasn't forgotten about you.

$\mathcal{F}$or dreams that look as though they'll take a lifetime to accomplish, get ready. It's going to happen sooner than you think. Things are about to fall into place.

*Y*our mind may say no, but if you'll listen down in your spirit,
you will hear that still, small voice
saying, "Yes, it is on the way."

*O*ne touch of [God's] favor will put you into overflow.

*G*od won't allow you to just be a giver. When you give,
it will come back to you good measure,
pressed down, and running over.

*P*itch your tent in the land of hope.

*G*et up every morning with expectancy, knowing that the
Most High God is working out His plan for your life.

You ou were not created to live in dysfunction, with addictions, and to be constantly struggling. That may be how it's been in the past, but that's not how it's going to be in the future.

*G*od's about to do a new thing.

*W*hy don't you do yourself a favor, pull up your stakes, pick up your tent, and move out of the land of doubt, negativity, and self-pity?

....

....

....

....

....

....

....

....

....

....

....

....

....

....

....

....

....

....

....

....

....

God can vindicate us better than we can vindicate ourselves.

*D*on't waste your time worrying. [God's] on the throne.

....
....
....
....
....
....
....
....
....
....
....
....
....
....
....
....
....
....
....
....
....
....
....

*B*e determined, pursue your dreams, but be smart enough to
realize that what God wants to be yours will come to you.

$\mathcal{D}$avid's father tried to convince Samuel to anoint one of his other seven sons. He thought David was too small, too young, too inexperienced. But no matter how hard he tried, Samuel wouldn't do it. God was showing us that what has your name on it won't go to anyone else.

*Y*ou can't open a door that God has closed.

*G*od doesn't choose the way people choose.
People look on the outside. God looks on the heart.

When something doesn't work out your way, it's because God has something better in store.

God is about to wake up what you thought was over and done....
Healing is on the way, freedom is on the way,
God's favor is on the way.

....
....
....
....
....
....
....
....
....
....
....
....
....
....
....
....
....
....
....
....
....

Abundance is on the way!

Ellie Claire
Hachette Book Group
1290 Avenue of the Americas, New York, NY 10104
ellieclaire.com

First edition: April 2020

Ellie Claire is a division of Hachette Book Group, Inc. The Ellie Claire name and logo are trademarks of Hachette Book Group, Inc.

Print book interior design by Bart Dawson.

ISBN: 9781546015277

Printed in China
RRD-S
10 9 8 7 6 5 4 3 2 1